NATURE'S FURY

FLOODS

Cari Meister

ABDO
& Daughters

Visit us at
www.abdopub.com

Published by ABDO Publishing Company, 4940 Viking Drive, Edina, MN 55435.
Copyright ©1999 by Abdo Consulting Group, Inc. International copyrights reserved
in all countries. No part of this book may be reproduced in any form without written
permission from the publisher.

Printed in the United States.

Edited by: Paul Joseph
Art Direction: John Hamilton
Contributing Editor: Morgan Hughes

Cover photo: AP/Wide World Photos
Interior photos: Digital Stock, page 5
                 Corbis, pages 1, 3, 4, 6, 8-16, 20-28, 31, 32

Sources: Lane, Frank W. *The Violent Earth.* Topsfield, Massachusetts: Salem House,
1986; Ludlum, David M. *The Audubon Society Field Guide to North American
Weather.* New York: Alfred A. Knopf, 1991; Robinson, Andrew. *Earth Shock.* New
York: Thames and Hudson, Ltd., 1993; Various articles on http://www.floodplain.org;
Various articles on http://www.nws.noaa.gov; Various articles on http://www.pbs.org/
wghh/nova/flood; Williams, Jack. *The Weather Book, Second Edition.* New York:
Random House, 1997.

Library of Congress Cataloging–in–Publication Data

Meister, Cari.
    Floods / Cari Meister
        p. cm. — (Nature's fury)
    Includes bibliographical references and index.
    Summary: Discusses the nature, causes, and dangers of floods, floods of the
past, and ways to survive them.
    ISBN 1-57765-082-4
    1. Floods—Juvenile literature. [1. Floods] I. Title. II. Series: Meister, Cari.
Nature's fury.
GB1399.M45 1999
551.48 '9—dc21   98-6648
                                                        CIP
                                                        AC

CONTENTS

In 1898, a family rows past a church in Minneapolis, Minnesota, during a flood of the Mississippi River.

FLOODS

ON SATURDAY, JULY 31, 1976, VISITORS TO BIG THOMPSON Canyon in Colorado were setting up camp. Bright-colored tents dotted the landscape. Inside the tents, kids rolled out their sleeping bags. Some probably put their flashlights right by their pillows, so that they'd be easy to find when it got dark. Families and friends sat around campfires. It had been cloudy all day. There were even threats of thunderstorms.

In other parts of the canyon, people were hiking. Some were driving through the beautiful scenery. People in canyon restaurants were just sitting down to dinner.

At 6:30 p.m. it began raining. Campers ducked into their tents. Hikers jumped into their cars. Some visitors thought they'd wait out the rain in a shop or restaurant. But the rain kept on coming. A huge thunderstorm cloud sat right on top of the canyon. The cloud didn't blow away. It stayed right on top of the canyon. It rained and rained and rained. Some radar screens showed that 10 to 12 inches (25 to 30 cm) of rain fell in only 90 minutes.

Hardly any of the rain soaked into the dirt. Rivers of water poured down the sides of the canyon. A monstrous wall of water formed. The wall rushed down on the unsuspecting visitors. At some places, the wall was over 19 feet (6 m) tall. It was so

Overflow of the Mississippi River in 1993.

4

A flash flood strikes
in west Texas.

A rescue worker scans the flood-swollen Big Thompson River for possible flood victims where the highway ends in the Big Thompson Canyon near Loveland, Colorado. The flash flood of 1976 killed 139 people.

powerful that it roared like a jet engine. The flood washed over campsites, restaurants, and shops. Boulders caught up in the rush tumbled down the canyon's sides, smashing cars and plowing over trees. Highways and roads were destroyed.

The storm hit suddenly and violently. There was not enough time to send out an official warning. Some people were lucky. They climbed to high places. People who stayed in their cars were doomed. The rocks and boulders smashed cars to pieces. The flood killed 139 people, some of whom were never found. Over 400 homes were demolished. About 50 businesses were destroyed. Total damage was estimated at $35.5 million.

Floods are very dangerous, especially flash floods. Flash floods, like the one at Big Thompson Canyon, happen fast. Other floods happen more slowly, over a period of weeks, months, and even years. Floods occur all over the world. They occur in cities, in towns, near rivers, and by coasts. A flood is defined as "a body of water that covers land not usually covered by water." Floods are the deadliest of all natural disasters. In the United States, about 200 people die every year in floods. Every year they cause about $2 billion worth of damage in the United States alone.

THE WATER CYCLE

WATER IS IMPORTANT TO ALL LIVING THINGS. WE DRINK IT. We use it to wash, to clean, and to grow food. Water covers about three-quarters of the earth's surface. About 97 percent of the world's water is in the oceans. The rest is in rivers, lakes, and streams. Water is usually not dangerous when it is controlled. But when water becomes unruly, it can be deadly. Floodwaters kill people all over the world every year. Floods destroy homes and crops. Some have wiped out entire villages.

Floodwaters are so dangerous for two main reasons. For one thing, water is very heavy. Heavy things can do a lot of damage. One gallon of water weighs 8.5 pounds (3.9 kg). A bathtub of water weighs three-quarters of a ton (.68 metric tons). Water gets more destructive as the speed of the flow increases. Think about a bucket of water. You can reach your hand in and swish the water around with very little energy. Now think about picking up the bucket. It's heavy! Now think about letting the water flow out, just a little at a time, on top of a tall sand castle. When your bucket is empty, part of the castle might still be there. Now, if you dumped the whole bucket on the castle at one time, the castle would

These huts are built to float during the annual floods in Cambodia.

A flash flood fills a gully, sending water and mud rushing into the Missouri River in central Montana.

disappear a lot faster. Heavy, fast-flowing water is destructive.

Another reason that floodwaters are so dangerous is that many people live near places that flood. Over half of the people in the world live near river deltas, river mouths, and oceans. This is not surprising. People need water. They need it to drink and to eat, and to make a living. Many farmers live near riverbanks because the soil is rich. People also use rivers to transport goods. They sometimes use a river's power to run factories.

People know that rivers overflow. They know that tsunamis (tidal waves) can crash into ocean shores. But, many people choose to live near rivers and oceans anyway—some for necessity and others for pleasure.

A man wades across a flooded street after a winter rainstorm in Nehalem, Oregon.

Floods happen every year. This is why: Every year, rain falls. Most of the rain evaporates into the air, or is absorbed by soil and plants. The rain that does not evaporate or soak into the earth runs into streams, rivers, lakes, and the ocean. Once it gets back to the ocean, it evaporates back into the air and the whole process starts again.

About two-thirds of rain evaporates. The rest of the water falls into two categories. Controllable runoff is water that flows into rivers and lakes. Controllable runoff does not cause floods. Uncontrollable runoff causes floods. Uncontrollable runoff flows towards the already-filled lakes and rivers. But because there is no space, it causes the rivers and lakes to overflow. Think of a bathtub. A bathtub, like a lake and river, can only hold so much water. If you leave the water running, it will run over the top of the tub, and cause a flood on your bathroom floor.

PREDICTING FLOODS

THERE ARE TWO MAIN KINDS OF FLOODS. SEASONAL floods are floods that happen at the same time every year. The Nile River in Africa used to overflow every year. Heavy rains meant that flooding occurred every August and September. People along the Nile counted on the flooding to help their crops. Today, a giant dam reduces flooding on the Nile. Parts of the Mississippi River would overflow every year, too, if humans didn't build things to stop the flooding. Seasonal floods are more controllable because we expect them. We can be prepared.

Flash floods are unexpected floods. There are many reasons why flash floods occur. Some flash floods occur when a lot of rain falls on the same spot. Flash floods can also be triggered if snow and ice melt quickly in an area already saturated with water. Sometimes, big objects like boulders and logs clog up rivers and cause flash floods. Sometimes when rivers change course, flash floods occur. Some rivers, like the Yellow River in China, carry a lot of silt. Some of the silt falls to the river's bottom. Over time, the silt builds up on the bottom of the river. This pushes the water higher and higher. A flood occurs when the water overflows the banks. Some flash floods are caused when dams and

A flash flood beginning in a swollen mountain creek.

An auto is buried in silt near Winona, Minnesota, after heavy rains in 1938 brought huge deposits of sand and mud from the bluffs of the nearby Mississippi River.

reservoirs break. Waters that were meant to be held break free. Flash floods are difficult to predict. Flash floods are often deadly surprises.

Hydrologists are people who study water and the effects of water on land. Hydrologists keep track of how much water is in lakes, streams and rivers. They take measurements of how much rain has fallen. They keep track of how much rain is expected. They test the soil to see how much more water the soil can hold. All of these tests help them determine if and when a flood might occur.

Hydrologists have many tools to help them monitor water levels. Radar helps show where and how much rain is falling. If a lot of rain is falling on an area, it may signal that a flash flood may occur.

A hydrologist for the U.S. Forest Service measures the amount of erosion created by a thunderstorm that occurred the day after a catastrophic firestorm.

Hydrologists use computers to plug in water numbers. Sometimes the math formulas already installed in the computers help warn hydrologists of floods. Stilling wells measure changes in a river or lake's height. Hydrologists also use many instruments for measuring changes in water content of soil and plants.

In addition, hydrologists are also in charge of watching dams and reservoirs. They make sure that they do not have cracks or holes that might cause them to break. Hydrologists also make sure that they're not close to overflowing.

If it looks as if a flood is coming, the National Weather Service will issue a flood watch or a flood warning. A flood warning is more serious than a flood watch.

DAMS, DIKES & RESERVOIRS

FLOODS CAN BE DISASTROUS, BUT THEY CAN ALSO BE useful. In many parts of the world, rain is seasonal. At certain times, like during spring, a lot of rain falls on one place. At other times during the year, the same place may suffer a drought. The excess rain, or floodwater, can be stored and used during times of drought.

People have been trying to control floodwater for centuries. About 2800 B.C. the Egyptians built the earliest known dam on the Nile River. Today, there are dams, dikes, and reservoirs all over the world. Dams, dikes, and reservoirs work to help control floodwaters. They provide storage areas for excess water. They hold back waters that might flood. They also free waters through rivers that might otherwise dry out.

A dam is a barrier that holds back the flow of water. There are many kinds of dams. Masonry dams are built of concrete and stone. A gravity dam is a type of masonry dam. A gravity dam is built of large blocks of concrete. Gravity dams are the biggest and strongest dams made today. A gravity dam holds back massive amounts of water. They are built on top of solid rock. The Shasta Dam is one of the tallest gravity dams in the United States. The Shasta Dam is located in California, on the Sacramento River.

This flood control dam with spillways helps control the flow of the Mississippi River.

The Shasta Dam in California, on the Sacramento River.

Embankment dams are built of rocks, sand, clay, and other things from the earth. An earth-fill dam is a type of embankment dam. It is made in layers. A layer of rock, sand, or clay is put into place. Huge, heavy rollers compact the layer. Another layer of rock, sand, or clay is put into place. The huge, heavy rollers come back and compact that layer. An earth-fill dam is made up of hundreds of layers. An earth-fill dam's outside walls are called riprap. Riprap protects the dam from ice, rain, and wind. Special materials are put in all the cracks to make sure water does not leak. The Rogun Dam in Tajikistan is the tallest dam in the world. It was finished in 1989, and stands 1,099 feet (335 m) tall.

A dike is a ditch or a bank that is used to funnel water out of unwanted areas. Dikes help stop floods by draining waters out of areas in danger of flooding. Dikes are usually made of materials from the earth.

Above: Lake Victoria, Africa.
Right: The Aswan Dam, Egypt, on the Nile River, 1902.

A reservoir is a place where large amounts of water are stored. Some reservoirs are natural lakes. Some reservoirs are made by people. Some reservoirs are formed when dams are constructed. Seasonal rainwater and floodwaters are channeled into reservoirs. There, water is held until needed. The largest reservoir in the world is Lake Victoria, in Africa.

Dams, dikes, and reservoirs are useful in controlling and using floodwaters. But they need to be watched closely at all times. Rot, cracks, and poor construction can cause them to burst open. About three dams burst every year. Bursting dams can cause disastrous flash floods. One such flash flood occurred in Johnstown, Pennsylvania, in 1889.

16

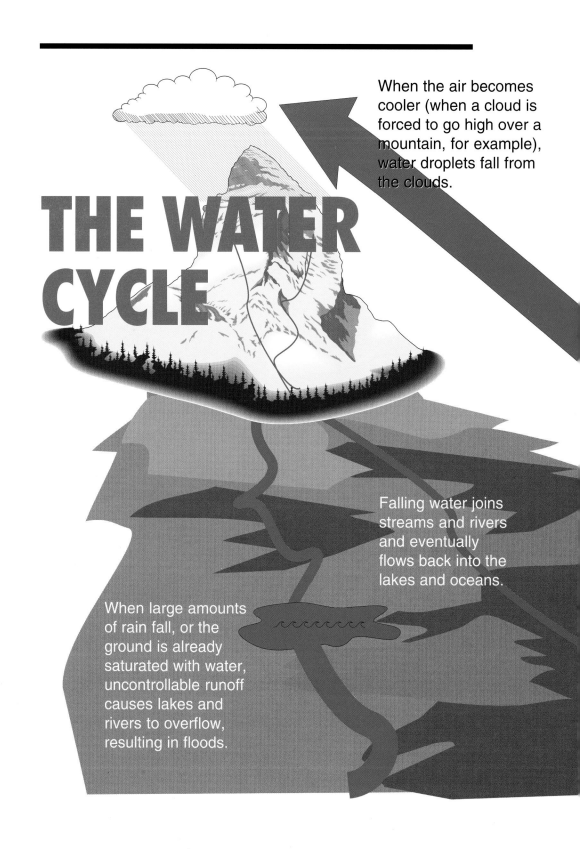

THE WATER CYCLE

When the air becomes cooler (when a cloud is forced to go high over a mountain, for example), water droplets fall from the clouds.

Falling water joins streams and rivers and eventually flows back into the lakes and oceans.

When large amounts of rain fall, or the ground is already saturated with water, uncontrollable runoff causes lakes and rivers to overflow, resulting in floods.

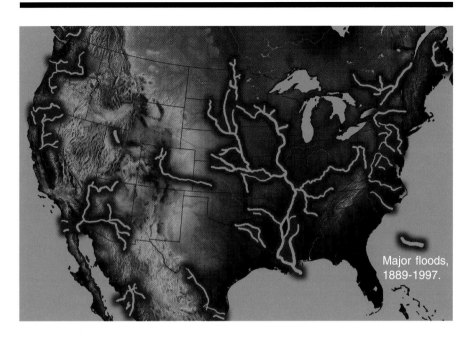

Major floods, 1889-1997.

Trees and other plants also release water vapor into the air, helping the clouds to gather more and more moisture.

According to the National Weather Service, in most years flooding causes more deaths and damage than any other natural disaster. In many years it is common for three-quarters of all Federal disaster declarations to be due, at least in part, to flooding.

Water evaporates from the oceans and other large bodies of water. Clouds form from the water vapor in the air.

FAMOUS FLOODS

ON MAY 31, 1889, PEOPLE IN JOHNSTOWN, PENNSYLVANIA, were going about their day. Some people were shopping. Some were working. Some people were probably looking out the window wishing that the rain would stop.

Then, all of a sudden, a huge wall of water about 150 feet (46 m) high crashed through the city. The wall came from South Fork, where

The scene at Johnstown, Pennsylvania, as the bridge is washed away during the flood of 1889.

it had already picked up trees, rock, and other debris. Houses were ripped apart. Trees were wrenched from the ground. A giant fire blazed through town. More than 2,000 people died. In addition, 565 children were left without one or both of their parents. The cause of the flood was from a dam that burst following a week of torrential rain.

The South Fork Dam was built in 1853. The dam's purpose was to bring water to the Pennsylvania Canal during dry spells. However, by the time it was completely built, it wasn't needed. The dam and reservoir lay unused for many years. It was in poor shape and in need of repair, but nobody seemed to notice until it was too late.

The aftermath of the great 1889 flood of Johnstown, Pennsylvania. More than 2,000 people perished.

In 1966, a flash flood ripped through Florence, Italy. It happened at night. People were all asleep in their beds. They had no idea a flood was coming. Then, later in the night they awoke to a low rumbling. The Arno River was flowing through the streets! It smashed into bridges. It flowed into shops. Then it made its way to the church of Santa Croce. Here it ran over ancient tombs of Galileo, Michelangelo, Machiavelli, and others and destroyed priceless works of art. The number of people who died was low, but the amount of damage was enormous. The flood was caused by improper monitoring of two dams located upstream.

In the fall of 1992 through the summer of 1993, record amounts of rain fell on the Midwest. Both the Mississippi and the Missouri rivers swelled. In some places, they poured over, flooding towns, farms, and houses. In other parts the rivers just kept getting higher and higher, threatening flood. Flooding along the Mississippi and

Missouri rivers in 1993 devastated nine states.

The flooding started in June, and lasted until August. An estimated 22,000 homes were damaged or destroyed. More than 85,000 people had to leave their homes for safer areas. The floods caused $20 billion in damage. It was not surprising that the rivers flooded. Rivers flood. It's a natural fact. Despite all of the dams and blockades humans make, rivers sometimes still flood. What made the floods of 1993 so incredible was that they lasted for three months. And, for the first time ever, both the Mississippi and the Missouri flooded at the same time.

The Yellow River in China floods more than any other river in the world. In the last 2,000 years it has flooded more than 1,000 times. That's once about every two years. The floods kill. In 1887, flooding on the Yellow River killed an estimated 900,000 people, dumped 20 to 30 feet (6 to 9 m) of water on 50,000 square miles (129,499 square km) of crop land, and left two million people homeless. In 1931, four million people died. In 1938, another million died. The Yellow River is often called "China's Sorrow."

Left: An aerial view of the Missouri River after the floods of 1993. The lowest regions are purple, and the highest are yellow. Water damage from levee failures can be seen in the bottom of the horizontal parts of the river curves.

A wrecked car is left by a statue in Florence, Italy, following the devastating flood of November 1966. The water of the Arno River rose as high as 20 feet (6m), submerging sculptures, paintings, mosaics, and manuscripts in the city's libraries.

STAYING SAFE

FLOODS ARE DANGEROUS. AS YOU ALREADY READ, THEY kill people every year. Never try to be a hero in a flood situation. Some floodwaters may be fairly calm, but sometimes they are deceiving. Sometimes flash floods come quickly. You might not have time to prepare for them.

The best thing to remember in a flash flood is to climb to safety. If you have time, grab a blanket, a flashlight and a battery-powered radio. The higher you are, the better. If you are in your house, climb to the second floor, or the roof. If you are outside, climb to the top of the nearest hill, building, or other structure. Never try to swim to safety. Climb to the highest spot you can and wait. Rescue teams will come looking for you. Many people have died trying to swim to safety in floods.

Sometimes flood warnings give you time to prepare for the flood. If you have time, there are other things you can do. But at the first sign of the flood, get to high ground! Floodwaters rise fast. In 1938, during a flood, a man crossed the street to get his child out of a car. When he crossed the street the first time, the water was up to his ankles. When

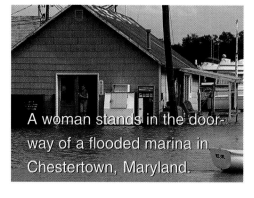

A woman stands in the doorway of a flooded marina in Chestertown, Maryland.

A flooded road in
Snohomish, Washington.

he crossed the street the second time, the water was up to his chest!

If you do have time, bring everything from outside, like lawn chairs, bikes, and toys, inside. Floating debris kills. You can also board up windows. If it is safe to evacuate by car, get your car ready. Collect cans of food, bottled water, blankets, a first-aid kit, dry clothing, flashlights, and medicines and put these in your car.

Other important things to remember:

- Listen to flood warnings. If told to leave, do so immediately.
- Do not walk through floodwater more than ankle deep.
- Do not drive with anyone if the roads are covered with water. Some cars will float in less than 12 inches (30 cm) of water.
- Do not walk over a bridge if there is any water on it.
- Do not touch electrical lines or cords.
- Do not raft or tube in swollen creeks or rivers.
- Floods that may look calm are not.

It is always a good idea to be prepared. If a flood struck suddenly, where would you go? How would you get there? It is important for all family members to know what to do in a flood.

CLEANING UP

IMAGINE WALKING BACK INTO YOUR HOUSE AFTER A flood. You wade through inches of muddy sludge. Everything is caked in mud and dirt. The couch. The picture of you and your sister on the wall. Even the blankets on your bed. Unknown objects float in the basement. Your dog whines at your side. At first he liked the water. Now he can't find his food dish.

Your mom is in the other room crying. Your dad is talking to the insurance agent on the phone. Everything is a mess. You try to remember that you were lucky. No one in your family was hurt. Your house is still standing. But it's hard.

The aftermath of floods are often devastating. People lose family heirlooms and other special things. It takes weeks to clean the mess. Some things are beyond cleaning. They just have to be thrown away. Before you even step into your house to start cleaning, make sure it's safe. Have an adult open the door. If the building looks like it might collapse, stay out! Once you get inside, do not turn on any lights or switches. Water and electricity are very dangerous when put together.

The first thing to do is to cover any windows or holes. The last

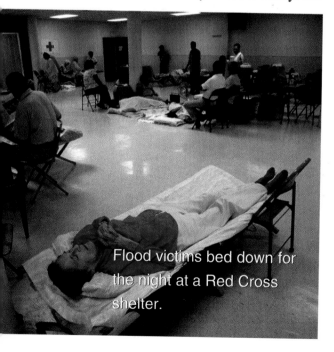

Flood victims bed down for the night at a Red Cross shelter.

A Red Cross worker and pilot
prepare for a nighttime blood
delivery in a helicopter.

thing you want is more damage. Throw away all foods and medicines that touched water. They could be spoiled. Do not use the water until your city or town has declared it safe to use. These are only a few of the things you need to consider when you move back home. Disaster relief agencies in your area can provide you with more information about cleaning up after a flood. They can tell you the best way to dry furniture. They can tell you how to get rid of mildew. They can tell you how to drain your flooded basement and a lot of other things.

The Red Cross is one disaster relief agency. The Salvation Army is another. Volunteers from these agencies are trained to help people cope with the aftermath of floods. They can help you. If your house is not livable, they can help you find a place to stay. If you don't have any dry clothes, they can help you find some. If you need food or medical care, they can help with that, too. There are many disaster relief agencies all over the United States. You can find which agencies are in your area by calling your city or village hall, or by looking in the phone book.

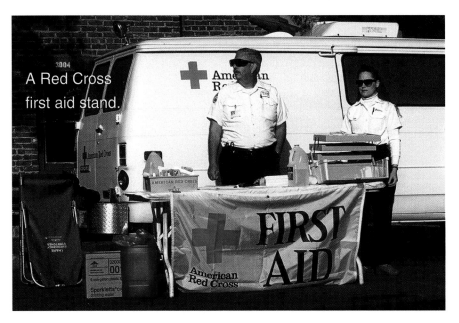

A Red Cross first aid stand.

INTERNET SITES

http://www.floodplain.org

The Floodplain Management Web site. Tons of information on floods and flood-prone areas.

http://www.nws.noaa.gov

The National Weather Service's official home page. Check out the latest flood conditions in your area.

http://www.pbs.org/wgbh/nova/flood

See photos of flooded regions all over the country. Find out more about the Nile River, the Yellow River and the Mississippi River.

These sites are subject to change. Go to your favorite search engine and type in "floods" for more sites.

PASS IT ON

Science buffs: educate readers around the country by passing on information you've learned about floods. Share your little-known facts and interesting stories. We want to hear from you!

To get posted on the ABDO Publishing Company Web site, E-mail us at "Science@abdopub.com"

Visit the ABDO Publishing Company Web site at:
www.abdopub.com

GLOSSARY

Dam: A barrier that holds back the flow of water.

Delta: The place at the mouth of a river where clay, sand, dirt or other material carried by the river collects.

Dike: A ditch or a bank used to funnel water out of unwanted areas.

Evaporate: To change into vapor.

Flash Floods: Floods that appear quickly.

Hydrologist: A person who studies water and the effects water has on land.

Mouth: The place where a river empties into the ocean, or a stream empties into a river.

National Weather Service: The service that collects weather statistics and issues storm warnings.

Reservoir: A place where water is stored.

Saturated: To fill up completely; soaked.

Seasonal Floods: Floods that occur at the same time every year.

Silt: Loose particles of rock.

Stilling Well: A large enclosure with small holes that let water flow in and out, used to measure water height.

A cyclist attempts to make his way through a water-logged street in Florence, Italy, following the devastating flood of November 1966.

INDEX